SACRED NOCTURNES

HEATHER SORENSON
PIANO

CONTENTS

PAGE 3 .... UNTITLED
PAGE 6 .... I WILL ARISE AND GO TO JESUS
PAGE 10 .... BE THOU MY VISION
PAGE 16 .... THIS IS MY FATHER'S WORLD
PAGE 21 .... AT DAY'S END
PAGE 25 .... SHALL WE GATHER AT THE RIVER
PAGE 29 .... A REFLECTION ON THE CROSS
PAGE 34 .... ALL THROUGH THE NIGHT
PAGE 40 .... BE STILL MY SOUL
PAGE 45 .... NEARER, MY GOD, TO THEE
PAGE 50 .... TURN YOUR EYES UPON JESUS
PAGE 52 .... 'TIL WE MEET AGAIN

Visit Shawnee Press Online at www.shawneepress.com/songbooks

GlorySound
A Division of Shawnee Press, Inc.
1107 17th Avenue South • Nashville, TN 37212

Copyright © 2008 GlorySound
A Division of Shawnee Press, Inc. International Copyright Secured. All Rights Reserved.
SOLE SELLING AGENT: SHAWNEE PRESS, INC., NASHVILLE, TN 37212

FOREWORD

I am always interested, and sometimes amused, at which direction my projects end up taking. While I usually have a general concept in mind when I begin, the end result is always a surprise to me! This book is no different. Each project is heavily influenced by the current backdrop of my life. I can look back on most of my arrangements and tell you whom my heart was burdened for that week, which movie I had just seen, or what lesson God was teaching me.

The writing of this project came at a very unique time in my life, with many out-of-the-ordinary factors. But by far, my greatest influences were conversations I had with God while I walked in the evenings. Because these conversations so intrinsically shaped this project, I have included some of them on a companion product enhanced CD to increase the interpretation of the music. It is my prayer that this book will be a tool that God uses to minister to you and through you.

Special Thanks to those who have "propped up my arms" this past year, to the friends who prayed without ceasing, and to all of my R.E.A.L. Life kids for bringing me joy!

HEATHER SORENSON

Over the years, Heather Sorenson's journey has led her through a wide spectrum of musical experiences, including music education, children's musical productions, orchestrating, and church music. She is best known, however, as a free-lance piano arranger, and her arrangements are becoming increasingly popular as competition pieces at the state and national levels. Heather also travels as a clinician, leading piano master classes and speaking at various worship conferences held throughout the country.

She currently resides in Dallas, Texas where she is the Music Associate at Lavon Drive Baptist Church. In her "free" time, Heather works with the youth at her church. Mentoring teenagers is her passion- most weekends find her camped out at Starbucks, solving all the world's problems with "her" kids.

UNTITLED

HEATHER SORENSON

Rubato, unhurried (♩ = ca. 104-112)

Copyright © 2008 GlorySound
(A Division of Shawnee Press, Inc., Nashville, TN 37212)
International Copyright Secured. All Rights Reserved.

Duplication of this publication is illegal, and duplication is not granted by the CCLI, LicenSing or OneLicense.net licenses.

I WILL ARISE AND GO TO JESUS

Tune: **RESTORATION**
Walker's Southern Harmony
Arranged by
HEATHER SORENSON

Rubato, with feeling (♩ = ca. 124-130)

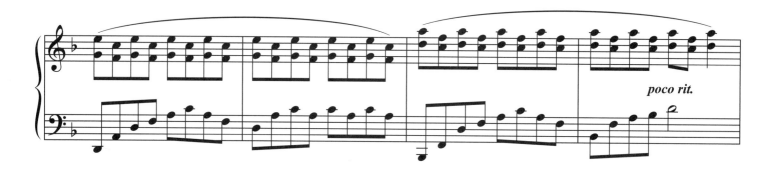

Copyright © 2008 GlorySound
(A Division of Shawnee Press, Inc., Nashville, TN 37212)
International Copyright Secured. All Rights Reserved.

Duplication of this publication is illegal, and duplication is not granted by the CCLI, LicenSing or OneLicense.net licenses.

HE5140

BE THOU MY VISION

Tune: **SLANE**
Traditional Irish Melody
Arranged by
HEATHER SORENSON

Copyright © 2008 GlorySound
(A Division of Shawnee Press, Inc., Nashville, TN 37212)
International Copyright Secured. All Rights Reserved.

Duplication of this publication is illegal, and duplication is not granted by the CCLI, LicenSing or OneLicense.net licenses.

HE5140

THIS IS MY FATHER'S WORLD

Tune: **TERRA PATRIS**
by Franklin L. Sheppard (1852-1930)
Arranged by
HEATHER SORENSON

Copyright © 2008 GlorySound
(A Division of Shawnee Press, Inc., Nashville, TN 37212)
International Copyright Secured. All Rights Reserved.

Duplication of this publication is illegal, and duplication is not granted
by the CCLI, LicenSing or OneLicense.net licenses.

AT DAY'S END

HEATHER SORENSON

SHALL WE GATHER AT THE RIVER

Tune: **HANSON PLACE**
by Robert Lowry (1826-1899)
Arranged by
HEATHER SORENSON

dedicated to Joni V.

A REFLECTION ON THE CROSS

Tune: **HAMBURG**
by Lowell Mason (1792-1872)
Arranged by
HEATHER SORENSON

Copyright © 2008 GlorySound
(A Division of Shawnee Press, Inc., Nashville, TN 37212)
International Copyright Secured. All Rights Reserved.

Duplication of this publication is illegal, and duplication is not granted by the CCLI, LicenSing or OneLicense.net licenses.

HE5140

ALL THROUGH THE NIGHT

Tune: **AR HYD Y NOS**
Traditional Welsh Melody
Arranged by
HEATHER SORENSON

Copyright © 2008 GlorySound
(A Division of Shawnee Press, Inc., Nashville, TN 37212)
International Copyright Secured. All Rights Reserved.

Duplication of this publication is illegal, and duplication is not granted by the CCLI, LicenSing or OneLicense.net licenses.

HE5140

Tune: **Country Gardens** by Percy Grainger

BE STILL MY SOUL

dedicated to Lynette O.

Tune: **FINLANDIA**
by Jean Sibelius (1865-1957)
Arranged by
HEATHER SORENSON

Copyright © 2008 GlorySound
(A Division of Shawnee Press, Inc., Nashville, TN 37212)
International Copyright Secured. All Rights Reserved.

Duplication of this publication is illegal, and duplication is not granted by the CCLI, LicenSing or OneLicense.net licenses.

HE5140

41

NEARER, MY GOD, TO THEE

Tune: **BETHANY**
by Lowell Mason (1792-1872)
Arranged by
HEATHER SORENSON

Copyright © 2008 GlorySound
(A Division of Shawnee Press, Inc., Nashville, TN 37212)
International Copyright Secured. All Rights Reserved.

**Duplication of this publication is illegal, and duplication is not granted
by the CCLI, LicenSing or OneLicense.net licenses.**

TURN YOUR EYES UPON JESUS

dedicated to Heather and Denny

Tune: **LEMMEL**
by Helen H. Lemmel (1864-1961)
Arranged by
HEATHER SORENSON

Copyright © 2008 GlorySound
(A Division of Shawnee Press, Inc., Nashville, TN 37212)
International Copyright Secured. All Rights Reserved.

Duplication of this publication is illegal, and duplication is not granted by the CCLI, LicenSing or OneLicense.net licenses.

51

* Pianist may segue from the end of measure 33 to the beginning of **"Til We Meet Again"**, if desired.

HE5140

dedicated to Amy Forstrom

'TIL WE MEET AGAIN

Tune: **GOD BE WITH YOU**
by William G. Tomer (1833-1896)
Arranged by
HEATHER SORENSON

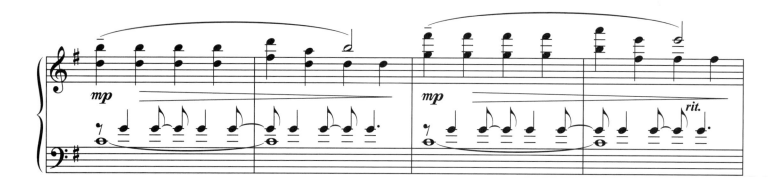

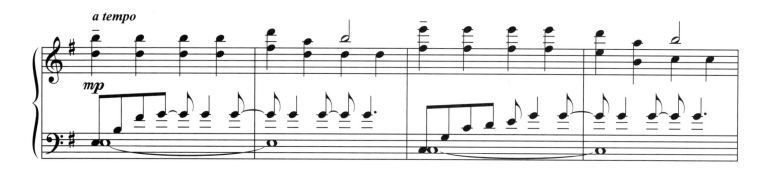

Copyright © 2008 GlorySound
(A Division of Shawnee Press, Inc., Nashville, TN 37212)
International Copyright Secured. All Rights Reserved.

**Duplication of this publication is illegal, and duplication is not granted
by the CCLI, LicenSing or OneLicense.net licenses.**

HE5140

55